Margaret Houser

Darlene Hershberger

He Is
Her Friend

He Is
Her Friend

**How a mother's commitment supported a journey
of friendship, marriage and happiness.**

Margaret Houser

ISBN Hardcover: 978-0-9977345-0-8

Printed in the United States of America

To Terry and Mary because they wanted to get married.
—Darlene

He is her friend,
he always was and
he always will be.

Contents

Foreword

I met Dan, Darlene and Margaret when I started to take my daughter, Stephanie, to Speaking for Ourselves meetings.

Margaret and I would chat about things that occurred since we saw each other last. If you ever talked to Margaret you probably heard her say, "I'm going to have to put that in the book." And, a lot of people are waiting for the book.

Initially, I thought the story would be about a couple, with an intellectual disability, who got married. As time went on I realized the book was going to be just as much about an everyday life advocate, Margaret, as it was about Dan and Darlene.

At 71 years old Margaret is still extremely busy with Dan and Darlene's Everyday Life. I asked her once if she thought there were things that she neglected or missed, in her life, because of the amount of time she spends taking care of other people. She said, "I have neglected cleaning out the medicine chest."

I can't imagine how differently Dan and Darlene's lives would have turned out without Margaret, I can only imagine how others' lives could have been, if they had someone like Margaret.

—Laurene Kohler

$\mathcal{D}$an and Darlene's story is an incredible one.

I couldn't think about Dan and Darlene without acknowledging the love, support and inspiration of their entire family. There is a family and, then, there is a FAMILY!

Through my connection with Speaking for Ourselves, I personally witnessed the love, dedication and incredible support of Dan and Darlene's entire family, especially Margaret, Darlene's Mother.

The family is most gracious in giving credit to the services and supports they receive through the system. In reality, there is no system that would have ever accomplished what Dan and Darlene have. They have used the system to plug a few holes and strengthen their foundation, but their foundation is rock solid and supports them in living life together to its fullest.

—Dan Sausman

Preface

Commitment, Hope and Happiness

Little by little I have guided Darlene and Dan through their life's journey. It has been one of my life's greatest and most rewarding experiences, I have truly been blessed.

Getting the most out of the education system, obtaining and keeping a job, taking them to and from work, taking them where they want to go and where they need to go, making a meal, taking care of a house and taking care of themselves; it all takes an everyday commitment.

Yes, sometimes the commitment does interfere with things, but I have always felt that somebody had to help them and I wanted to be the one that did.

I have gotten to know many people, who are intellectually disabled, who want to be with that special someone; want to be married. My hope is that parents will give their children the opportunity to be with that special someone. They deserve to be together just like we deserve to be with our spouses. For me, supporting Darlene and Dan's desire to marry was the most difficult decision I ever had to make.

Acknowledgments

Miss Mary Kay Lemon, Donna Thompson, Betsy Richard, Dave Schreffler, Terri Stickle, Shannon Rexrode, Teresa Strickland, Gracie Bell, Rocco Cambria, Gerry Miner, Richard Updegraff, Carolyn Luddy, Dan Sausman, Amanda Harclerode, Dave Judy, Lou Whittle, Kate and Harry Kerstetter, Jay and Carol Wilsbach, Commissioner George Hartwick, John Wilsbach, Mark French, Janet Cambria, Richard Honeycutt, Charles (Chuck) Kray, Laurene Kohler, Jim White, Mrs. Ebersol, Capital Area Intermediate Unit, Compass Group/Canteen/Con-Ven-Co, Section 125 at the Hershey Bears hockey games, Speaking for Ourselves and its members, Camp Hope, Middletown Church of God, Wednesday Night Live group, Dan's family, Darlene's family, AHEDD, the Dauphin County Case Management Unit, JoAnn Bowles and Jean Hershberger.

Abbreviations and Definitions

AHEDD – A private, non-profit organization with a mission to serve the community as a catalyst in the employment and development of people with disabilities.

CMU – Case Management Unit - provides community-based services for children, young people, adults and families in Dauphin County. Provided services are in the areas of intellectual disabilities, mental health and early intervention.

Darlene – Quote from Darlene

Dan – Quote from Dan

Everyday Life – Everyday Lives is the core philosophy and framework of the State of Pennsylvania's Office of Developmental Programs (ODP). Originally introduced in 1991, Everyday Lives is deeply rooted in the concept of Self-Determination and Positive Approaches.

The fundamental concept of Everyday Lives is that, with the support of family and friends, individuals with disabilities decide how to live their lives and what supports they need.

It also means that they are responsible for their decisions and actions.

IU – Intermediate Unit - regional educational service agencies, established to serve a given geographic area's educational needs.

SFO – Speaking for Ourselves - Purpose is to help our members run their organizations, develop leadership skills through real-life experiences, learn to work together collectively to address their own issues, and increase their own self-sufficiency and independence.

Mission – to be an independent community organization controlled by people with disabilities who help us:

- Find a voice for ourselves

- Teach the public about the needs, wishes, and potential of people with disabilities

- Speak out on important issues

- Support each other through sharing, leadership development, and helping and encouraging each other

Supports Coordinator – Supports Coordinators assist in service choices, coordinate supports and monitor delivery of services within budgetary constraints.

1

Family Introductions

$\mathcal{I}$ am Darlene's mother, Margaret Houser, and Darlene's father is Butch Houser. We married in March of 1965 after Butch completed his military obligation in the Naval Reserve. Together we have 3 children: Darlene, Jeffrey and Anita.

Terry and Norma Hershberger were Dan's mother and father. They had 5 boys: Terry, Scott, Harold, Jeff, and Dan. Dan was born on June 29, 1963. Both of Dan's parents have passed away and I don't know much about their background. Dan's step mother, Jean, is still living and continues to have a relationship with Dan.

Walter N. Houser, Jr. (My Husband, Butch)

Butch was born on November 7, 1943 in Harrisburg, Pennsylvania to Walter N. and Ruth E. Houser, Sr. Butch has one older brother, Norman L. Houser, who was born in 1939.

For the first fourteen years of Butch's life his family lived in a first floor apartment of a large apartment complex. There was always someone to play with and always something to do.

1

Butch's father worked at the Bethlehem Steel Mill, in Steelton, Pennsylvania. His mother worked several part-time jobs outside the home.

While in high school Butch worked part-time at a 5 & 10 variety store and graduated from the Steelton-Highspire School District in 1961.

Butch enlisted in the U.S. Naval Reserve while in high school and started to attend monthly Naval Reserve drills between his junior and senior years. During active duty Butch was on the USS Rigel AF 58 during the Cuban Missile Crisis and also served on the USS Chikaskia AO-54.

After being discharged from the Navy, Butch returned home and worked full time at the 5 & 10. (This is where we met.) Butch also worked for the Glen Gery Brick Corporation for 10 years and was a mail carrier for the U.S. Post Office for 30 years.

Margaret Houser

I was born September 6, 1944 to Emma and Glenn Dintaman. I was the second of six children and had one sister and four brothers.

My older brother Glenn was brain damaged after falling out of his high chair as a baby.

Due to Glenn's limited ability my father treated me as the oldest child.

Even though Glenn was a year behind me in school we were in the same classroom. After a while the school separated us because I "looked after him too much."

Glenn is still alive. He is married and has 3 girls. His wife's brother was an auto mechanic and Glenn made a living working for his brother-in-law.

My parents were hard working people. My mother did washing and ironing, for other people, in our home. My father was a delivery driver for Wilsbach Distributors and worked for other businesses in his extra time.

I also worked very hard. Before going to school each morning I was expected to get my brothers and sister out of bed, make them breakfast, and get them ready for the day. I helped prepare dinner and cleaned up afterward each evening. If my mother's ironing was not done for the day, after school, I would help her finish. I couldn't participate in any extracurricular activities because my mother depended on me. I was always mother's helper.

I was very hurt when my mother, right in front of me, would tell people that she would have rather had six boys. I didn't understand this since I helped her so much.

Saturdays were spent cleaning the house and occasionally I would clean other people's houses, pass newspapers, and sell soft pretzels with my cousin.

On Sunday after church, the entire family would sit down for dinner together. After dinner we would visit Nanny, go for a ride in the car and stop for ice cream.

I was a good student and graduated from William Penn Senior High School in 1962. I wanted to be a nurse, but in my family when you graduated from high school, you got a job. There was no money for college.

I was a secretary for the Tri-County United Fund in Harrisburg for 3 years. Most of the time I walked to and from work because I did not want to spend money for bus transportation.

I met my husband, Butch, in 1963. We married in March of 1965 and bought our home, in Middletown, in July of 1965. We still live there today.

We were blessed with 3 children: Darlene in February of 1966, Jeffrey in October of 1968 and Anita in February of 1972.

I feel we were parents that worked hard to raise our children. We did, and wanted, what was best for them.

It was not always easy for the family to deal with a special needs child. We had our struggles but, through God, were able to get each of our children where they are today. Darlene is married, has a job and owns her own home. Jeffrey and Anita both have degrees, have jobs and are raising children of their own.

Butch and I are the proud grandparents to seven granddaughters.

Dan's Parents

I don't know very much about Dan's parents or Dan's life before we met him.

2
Darlene

Darlene's Birth

Darlene was born February 19, 1966. She weighed almost 9 pounds and there were no complications during the delivery. Everything seemed fine. She seemed healthy and gave a lusty cry after birth.

In those days, the baby was placed in a nursery and was not in the room with their mother. It was also a time when mother and baby stayed in the hospital for five or six days.

I was going to breast feed Darlene, but when the time came, they told me that Darlene had been put on oxygen. They had found Darlene gasping for breath and had turned blue.

During the 6 day hospital stay, I did not get to hold, feed, or diaper Darlene. Most of the time Darlene was in an oxygen tent.

There came a time when I knew something was not right, I didn't know what was wrong or what was causing the problem.

Darlene was my first child and I had no idea what was in our future. I was happy to have a beautiful little girl.

She was the first granddaughter on Butch's side of the family.

Darlene as a Toddler

Darlene was a good baby. She seemed ok but when she started to get around I thought, something is just not right with this kid. Butch didn't have any younger brothers or sisters and he didn't see that anything was not right.

I took Darlene to the doctors regularly and they never said anything about a developmental delay or brain damage that occurred during birth.

However, I knew things just weren't right. Red was green and green was red. She didn't comprehend yes and no and she had no fear of playing in the street, even after being disciplined. Darlene was very difficult at ages two and three.

I fudged on our grocery budget to get the money to send Darlene to nursery school. I felt it would do her some good to be around other children and it gave me a little break from our daily routine.

I enrolled Darlene in a neighborhood nursery school. She went two hours a day three times a week. According to the teacher, "Darlene was in her own little world and did not enter into group play."

Not knowing what the problem was, and being a first time mother, I just did my best.

Somehow through God's guidance we did well.

3
School Years

Kindergarten

So, off to school she goes.

Within a month, the teacher also felt that something was not right and requested that a psychological evaluation be performed.

The first question the psychologist asked us was, "was there a problem at birth?" I told her that the birth was uneventful, in fact the birth was easy for me, but there were complications afterward where Darlene was in an oxygen tent for a week. The diagnosis of the psychologist was that Darlene had brain damage and she would probably reach the mentality of a 10 or 12 year old.

I had suspicions early on so I was more prepared for the diagnosis than my husband. Butch reacted with denial and said they were full of crap.

Darlene – "Even though I had problems at birth I am like an average person."

The kindergarten teacher said she would keep Darlene in the classroom for the year and monitor how she progressed.

Butch and I felt it was good for Darlene to be around other children and the children accepted her as she was.

There was not much progress the first year and the teacher suggested that Darlene repeat kindergarten. There was progress the second year, but not enough so the teacher suggested that Darlene attend the Intermediate Unit for first grade.

First Grade

When first grade was almost over the teacher asked why Darlene came to the Intermediate Unit. The teacher felt that Darlene was too high functioning and the decision had been made that Darlene had to go back to our school district for second grade.

When you first meet Darlene and just look at her, she looks like an average person, and that's what makes things so difficult. Many people, and the teachers, just looked at her like an average person, and that's what they expect.

Second Through Eleventh Grade

Academically Darlene was able to pass all of her classes. Socially, she was not accepted and the kids picked on her. She did not make one lasting friendship.

High School Candy Bar Fundraiser

There was a candy bar fund raiser, and of course Darlene wanted to be part of it.

I helped her and when the event was over we sent in the money that Darlene had collected.

Afterward, I got a call from someone on the fund raising committee. They said Darlene still owed money. They went on to tell me that the candy bars were a dollar and Darlene had been selling them for fifty cents. I said, "And you knew that and you left her! You literally watched her sell candy bars that were supposed to be a dollar, for fifty cents, and now you are calling me to tell me she owes money." We came to an agreement that I would pay half of what was owed and Darlene would not participate in any other fund raisers.

The kids knew the candy bars were $1.00 and took advantage of Darlene.

Darlene Sat Out in the Hall Most of the Year

The year was almost over and I mentioned to Butch that we had not been called down to the school yet and Darlene said everything was okay.

Finally, we were called to the school. The teacher asked if we knew that Darlene sat out in the hall most of the year. Well, of course we didn't know, how would we have known? Darlene certainly didn't tell us! I told the teacher it was easier for them to let Darlene sit in the hall than work with her.

I can only wonder what occurred to make Darlene decide not to go into the classroom.

Darlene – "The kids would pick on me. They would mistreat me. They weren't treating me right."

Talk to Your Kids

Darlene wanted to walk home from school just like the other kids in the neighborhood.

One day it was late and she wasn't home yet. I went looking for her and found her up the street. A group of kids were beating her up, they nearly broke her arm.

Butch went to speak with the parents, but they pushed him out of their homes saying their child would not beat anyone up unless something was said that shouldn't have been said.

It's Almost Time to Graduate from High School

When Darlene was in the eleventh grade I was panicking. The school was going to let her graduate without any skills. I worked so hard with her all these years, but I thought I could not get her a job and provide the support she would need to keep a job. I couldn't have her stay at home just rocking on a chair. The situation was not good for her and it was not good for me.

Butch always said, "Darlene has two good arms and two good legs", expecting her to get a job someday. I really felt pressured.

Even though Darlene was registered with the Case Management Unit at the county, we had no contact with any Supports Coordinator. I guess the Case Management Unit expected the public school system to guide us because Darlene was still in school. The public school system did the best they could, I guess, but their specialty seemed to be normal children, not children with intellectual disabilities.

We were called to the school many times throughout the years and I would tell Butch, "They aren't telling us anything we don't already know, but they aren't telling us what to do." We were the only support system that Darlene had and there was no support system for us.

Darlene – "If it wasn't for Dan Sausman, we wouldn't have Speaking for Ourselves right now."

Back to the Intermediate Unit After the Eleventh Grade

At the end of the eleventh grade we were called over to the school once again. This time the teacher asked us if we knew about the program at the Intermediate Unit. I told her when Darlene was in first grade she attended the Intermediate Unit for a year and then was told that she was too high functioning to attend the following year. The teacher urged us to look at the current program at the Intermediate Unit.

Darlene – "That was Mrs. Ebersol mom. She was the one who said about me going to that special school."

Fortunately, the teacher went ahead and made an appointment for us with the Intermediate Unit superintendent.

Students were able to attend the Intermediate Unit until they were twenty-one, so Darlene would have three more years of school. The focus would be on everyday skills and often they helped with job placement after graduation.

All the students who attended had some sort of disability, some worse than others.

A school bus would pick Darlene up and drop her off at home. The transportation gave me peace of mind knowing that Darlene would be safe on the way to and from school.

If Darlene didn't like the school, she could stop attending, but she couldn't go back to her high school.

There were some things that we didn't like about the Intermediate Unit, but I told Butch, "She is going to come out of school and, like you say, she has two good arms and two good legs. I don't think I can get her a job. What is she going to do?" I decided we would give the Intermediate Unit a try.

Finally, from that point forward I got meaningful guidance from the school and the Case Management Unit.

Darlene – "That's where I met Dan. That's where I met my husband. That was Dan's last year and I was going in there. Dan said he was waiting until I graduated, that we would get out and be together."

Darlene loved the IU!

Again, Darlene was a high functioning student. This time the difference was that the teachers and aides asked Darlene to help with all sorts of things. Darlene liked being kept busy, she felt useful.

Darlene was accepted at this school: all the students were accepted. It was just like a family.

Each summer the school got her a job for six weeks. The first summer Darlene worked at a day care center. This didn't go very well and the staff reported that Darlene acted like the kids.

The next summer she worked at the library.

The last summer she worked in the laundry of a hospital and that was the best job experience to date.

Darlene – "I liked it but I didn't like the bloody sheets."

I provided transportation to and from all of these jobs.

The Intermediate Unit was a turning point in Darlene's life. Her skills were being developed, she enjoyed attending the school, she had friends, and she got exposure to different job experiences.

Darlene Met Dan at the Intermediate Unit

It was Dan's last year at the IU and Darlene's first year. Dan always went to the Intermediate Unit.

I went with Darlene on her first day at the IU. The teacher introduced Darlene to the class and asked the students to introduce themselves. When Dan stood up, he said, "I have a girlfriend named Sharon." I remember thinking, "Boy it would be so great if Darlene would meet somebody like Dan."

It wasn't long before Sharon went by the wayside. Dan said, "When I saw Darlene, I knew right then and there that Darlene was good looking and she was going to be my girlfriend."

They dated for Darlene's last three years of school. It was during this time that Dan, slowly, became part of our family.

After Graduation

I didn't want Darlene to work at Good Will because I thought she was more capable than what they required and she would get stuck there. The school advised that I let her go because she could possibly get picked up by another employer and it would be better than sitting at home.

The school was right. Two or three months after starting at Good Will, Darlene was offered a full time job as a housekeeper at a major hotel chain. The Case Management Unit and AHEDD assigned a job coach to support Darlene at work. Darlene is still employed at that hotel today.

I am so thankful for all the support and guidance that we received from the Intermediate Unit, the Case Management Unit and AHEDD job coach services. I know I could not have done it myself.

Working at the Hotel

Darlene is very particular about things. While cleaning rooms she would become focused on one thing, forgetting other things and it took longer to clean a room than the hotel expected. They found Darlene did much better working on a team and she was an excellent bed maker.

The hotel was very busy and they assigned Darlene to the laundry. They could see that Darlene was able to follow all the directions and was able to complete all the assigned tasks in the laundry. Darlene excelled in the laundry area.

The Big Tip

Someone left a $100.00 bill as a tip on the dresser of a room that Darlene cleaned.

Darlene knew this was a lot of money and didn't tell anyone about the tip except Dan. Dan told the job coach while showing her the new watch that Darlene had purchased for him. The job coach in turn discussed the tip with the hotel management.

Darlene was suspended for three 3 days while an investigation could be done to determine if this large sum of money was in fact a tip. The hotel needed to know if a customer unintentionally laid the money down, if someone lost the money, or if it was stolen. Where did it come from? The hotel's opinion was that NOBODY leaves a $100.00 tip.

After three days there was no word from the hotel, so Darlene went back to work. Upon her arrival a representative from the hotel asked what she was doing there. At this time, Darlene was told that she couldn't work at the hotel anymore.

Butch contacted the hotel to find out what the results of their investigation were and why Darlene was fired. The hotel representative said that Darlene stole the money. Butch informed them that they better have proof of the accusation and that his lawyer would be contacting them.

The hotel then scheduled a meeting with the job coach, not Butch, not me, and not Darlene.

The results of the investigation were:

- No guests could be contacted because the hotel didn't know what room number the money came from
- Darlene couldn't remember what room or what day she found the money
- No one called to report the money as lost or stolen

Darlene got her job back.

Work Problems

Complaints about Darlene's behavior occur almost daily when the job coach isn't at the hotel.

A new supervisor was hired and the general manager thought it would be a good idea for me to meet the new supervisor. This was a wonderful idea.

We met and I told her Darlene gets very flustered when she is overwhelmed and you need to let her know where you stand. She has been in the laundry for awhile and could probably run it herself if they would let her.

If I don't inform the supervisor who will? They won't listen to Darlene. I have to be on top of things.

At the meeting I took the opportunity to advocate for a change in Darlene's weekend work schedule. Darlene has worked both Saturday and Sunday for years but that's not the problem. We wanted her start and stop times changed by an hour.

I told the new supervisor that Darlene has been at the hotel for twenty-eight years. She shows up every day and you know she is going to be here and on time. Why, on the weekends, can't she work from 8:00 to 4:30? Darlene was working from 9:00 to 5:30.

The supervisor emailed us telling us that she had approved the start and stop time change. The change was an, "on again, off again" situation for a while, but now Darlene works 8:00 to 4:30 every day, not just on the weekends. It has been that way for a while now.

No Touching

The hotel called Butch and me to inform us that there was an incident and asked if we would attend a meeting at the hotel.

The job coach was made aware of the incident but, due to a new privacy policy, would not discuss it with me. Of course, it would be my responsibility to have the legal documentation drawn up to allow them to discuss things with me that we had openly discussed for the last twenty eight years. So, I asked Darlene what happened.

The general manager, human resources, the job coach, Darlene, Butch and I attended the meeting.

The general manager was very stern in starting the meeting, stating "I like Darlene, and she seems to do a good job. But, the hotel has rules and regulations." Then he asked Darlene to tell everyone what happened. (It bothered me that he said, "Seems to do a good job" rather than does a good job.)

Darlene said, "The houseman used that real bad F word to me and I told him he was to mind his own business. I yanked his hand out of the washer."

On the day in question Darlene was in the laundry area all by herself and was overwhelmed with the quantity of laundry that needed to be done. The hotel was very busy.

The housemen were coming in to the laundry yelling, I need towels, I need this, I need that. One houseman looked into a washer and yelled to Darlene that she didn't have enough towels in the washer and then proceeded to stuff additional towels in to the washer. Darlene took his hand and pulled his arm out of the washer.

The general manager said, "The hotel has a policy of no touching. Darlene was wrong to pull the houseman's hand out of the washer."

I wanted to know if the housemen were allowed in the laundry area and if they had the authority to tell Darlene what to do. The general manager refused to discuss anything about any other employees.

At the end of the meeting Butch asked what they were going to do and told them he was not going to let twenty-six years of employment end without doing what needed to be done. He also stated his frustration about the general manager's refusal to discuss the houseman's job responsibilities.

The meeting ended by the general manager looking directly at me and saying, "I will let everyone know what we are going to do by the end of the day. "

Later that day we got a call, Darlene was given a two week suspension without pay. The other employees were not discussed, but we later heard they were counseled, but not suspended.

When Darlene went back to work, everything was fine.

Full Time or Part-Time

Darlene was not being scheduled for a forty hour work week. The job coach questioned the situation and was told there was not enough work at the hotel to schedule Darlene for a full work week. My philosophy was that the lobby needed to be kept clean, the public area bathrooms needed to be kept clean, and the laundry area was still operating. There was still work that needed to be done.

I called to talk to the general manager and was assured that Darlene's hours would be increased on the next schedule, however three months later there was still no increase in hours.

I was very frustrated and didn't know what to do or who to talk to. So, I opened the phone book and browsed the yellow pages until I found a listing for human resources. I don't know if I got ahold of a government agency or a private agency, all I know is that I got ahold of somebody. At this point I didn't care if it was the right number or not, at least I could talk to someone about the situation.

After a few calls I finally found someone who could help us. They told me that since Darlene was hired as a full time employee, she could collect unemployment compensation for lost hours, if she worked less than thirty-two hours a week. This would only go back for the past six weeks. The person I talked to wanted to know why I waited so long to call someone.

Butch took care of the application process online.

Ever since, Darlene has been scheduled for at least thirty-two hours a week. Except for last week, the supervisor is new and she didn't know.

Benefits

The hotel where Darlene works has changed hands a number of times since she started to work there. The last chain to take over the hotel, took her: health insurance, vacation and retirement away. They just stopped all benefits, she just had a job.

After the first year they did honor her years of service and gave her vacation days.

4
Dan

*D*an's story starts around the first time that we met him.

Family

Dan's parent's names were Terry and Norma Hershberger. Dan has four brothers: Terry, Scott, Harold and Jeff. Dan is the youngest, he was born June 29, 1963.

Dan's mother died of a stroke suddenly when Dan was sixteen. She was in her fifties. Dan remembers being pulled out of school and being told about his mother's death.

The sudden death was very traumatic for Dan's dad, Terry. The people closest to Dan were afraid that Terry would not be able to take care of Dan.

Arrangements were made for Dan to live with one of his teachers from school. After a while he went to live with his oldest brother and, eventually, went back to live with his father.

Dee is Dan's oldest brother's wife. She has been very helpful to me. She is so thankful for the care I have given Dan.

Group Home Opportunity

The Case Management Unit talked to Dan about moving into a group home after he graduated from the Intermediate Unit. There would be at least two or three other people living there and a rotating staff to support everyday needs and activities.

Every time the subject came up Dan would tell them that he was not going to a group home, he was going to marry his girlfriend when she got out of school.

I thought, "Oh yeah, sure."

Money Management

After Dan graduated from the Intermediate Unit he got a job at a local department store.

The Saturday after payday a friend of Dan's, who could drive, would take him to the bank so Dan could cash his paycheck. Dan would buy his friend lunch and then his friend would drive Dan to our house.

After a few shopping trips, where Dan showered Darlene with gifts, I could see that Dan was wasting his hard earned money. I asked Dan if anyone helped him with his money and he told me he could do whatever he wanted with his money.

At this point, I accepted Dan as a son. I started to guide him by asking how he felt about opening up a savings account at a bank. I told him he could not continue to spend his paychecks on Darlene.

I did not want Dan's father to think I was trying to take Dan's money so I insisted that Terry sign the bank paperwork. My name was not on the account. Butch always insisted that Darlene and Dan's money be kept separate from ours and in accounts of their own.

After opening the savings account, I started to help Dan; whatever the need.

Job Problems

After leaving the department store Dan obtained employment where he washed pots and pans.

The job coach called and said Dan was being suspended for three days. I thought this was strange because it was the first time I was informed that Dan was not doing his job properly.

We went to Hershey Park for the day and were standing in line at the amphitheater when a lady came over to Dan and asked him how he was doing. I did not know the lady and Dan introduced us. They worked at the same place, but not in the same department.

I told the lady about Dan's suspension and the lady said, "I hear how they talk to Dan and I've seen how they mistreat Dan verbally. They cuss at him." You can imagine how I felt. I told the lady that I was so frustrated and that I didn't know what I could do. The lady said, "I'll tell you what to do. You go up to the human resources office on Seventh Street, and tell them just what happened."

I found the office in the phone book and called to make an appointment. They told me that before the appointment we needed to go to a district justice's office and fill out papers saying that Dan gave me permission to speak for him.

We were at the appointment for several hours. They asked many questions. Dan did say that they yelled at him and he thought he was doing his job right.

I think it was within two weeks that we got a call from human resources. They said they had talked to the supervisor and the person in charge at Dan's place of employment. Dan's employer would like to know what they can do to make this right.

I told them, "I don't think it is fair that you suspended Dan without pay. He should be paid for those three days and there should be no record in his permanent file. If you were having problems with Dan, all you needed to do was tell the job coach, that's why the job coach is there."

Within a day or so the employer responded saying they would remove the suspension from his file, they would pay him for the three days and they would keep in touch with the job coach. They have kept their word.

Dan - "Not only did AHEDD help me get the job I wanted but they are there for me when I need help."

5

The Relationship

The Beginning

*W*hen we met Dan he lived close to the Hershey Chocolate Factory in Hershey, Pennsylvania. It is at least eight miles from where we live.

At first, Dan would come to the house every Saturday morning. He would either walk or get a ride with someone. Can you believe that?

Stores and restaurants are within walking distance of my home, so Darlene and Dan would go shopping or eat at fast food restaurants by themselves. I would take them to the movies and keep track of them.

I started transporting Dan back and forth from his home. I called Terry a number of times to ask if he would come and pick Dan up and he would always say no.

Butch was very upset with me and would say, "Darlene is your first priority. Darlene is not everybody else's first priority. Why, why are you doing this when you have your hands full with what you have?"

It was a difficult time for me. I had 2 younger children and my husband felt I had my hands full with our family. Butch couldn't understand why I took on the responsibilities of another individual. I told Butch, "Dan is always good with her and I never have to worry about him mistreating her. He is her friend."

The Straw That Broke My Back

Darlene and Dan were both out of high school and both had been working at their jobs for a while.

Early in the relationship we got Darlene a phone in her room because she just loved talking to Dan. They talked for hours. Eventually it got to the point where Darlene would call for Dan and if he wasn't home she would get very upset. This was before cell phones.

Every time we did anything as a family, Dan went along. In fact, Darlene did not want to go on any family events without Dan. She refused to leave the house unless he was with us and I didn't want to leave her home alone. Since Dan didn't live with us it got harder and harder to get everyone to the right place at the right time.

This particular evening we all were going out to eat and to a hockey game.

Darlene had been trying to get Dan on the phone all day, but couldn't. She was very upset. Finally, I called Dan's house. Terry answered the phone. I said, "This is Margaret Houser, Darlene's mother, is Dan home or where is Dan? Darlene has been trying to get him all day." Terry said, "Dan has not been home for the whole weekend, I thought he was at your house." I responded by saying, "Mr. Hershberger, I would never have Dan at my house for the weekend unless you would know about it." Terry said, "Well, I don't have any idea where he is. Dan is more or less on his own. He doesn't cause any trouble." And I thought, "They just leave Dan fend for himself."

Everyone was worried because Dan was not at the house and it was time to leave for the hockey game. Nobody knew where he was.

Darlene was adamant that she was not going without Dan. Then Butch all but dragged Darlene down the steps of the house and out to the car. I told Darlene that she needed to go along and her behavior was ridiculous. Everybody was upset.

Just then around the corner comes Dan. I said, "Where in the HELL were you?"

Dan explained that he was staying with a family that lived up the street from us. They had a daughter with some kind of disability.

We all got in the car and off we went. Nobody enjoyed themselves, everybody was so upset.

This was not the first time things got out of control between Butch and Darlene but it was the worst. There were other times when Darlene would not go without Dan.

27

This incident was the straw that broke the camel's back.

That night I came home from the hockey game and thought, "I just can't live like this anymore, this is terrible, and she wants Dan here with her."

So, I made a decision. I told Darlene and Dan I was going to let them live together in an apartment. They said, "That would be great!" They had no fear.

I still remember Anita sitting on the floor listening when I told them. Anita said, "Are you crazy? I can't believe you are doing this Mom." I said, "Yes I am. I am literally here in the middle. Your Daddy feels I have enough to take care of without Dan. He can't see why I would transport Dan back and forth from his house to ours, to the bank, take them out to the movies, to the mall, or out to eat."

Because of my life experiences I never pushed my Darlene responsibilities off on to my other two children; I was very careful not to do that.

Everything was such a hassle for Butch and me.

It was the hardest thing I ever did when I decided to put them out into their own apartment. Even today I cannot believe that I made that decision. I just felt that Darlene should be with Dan.

Living Together

Butch and I found an efficiency apartment in an apartment complex. Once the application was approved, Darlene and Dan signed the lease themselves.

When they moved in Dan didn't have a lot, just his trophies and his clothes. I felt bad because he had so little.

They were fine, however, I was a wreck. I immediately got depressed. I kept thinking, "Darlene doesn't know how to cook. Darlene doesn't know how to clean." I cried a lot.

One night the fire whistle went off at 3:00 in the morning. Out of bed I go, and got dressed. Butch said, "Where are you going?" I said, "Over to Darlene's house to check on them." I got there and knocked on the door. Darlene answered and said, "Mom, what do you want?" I said, "Okay, good night."

Then, Butch said one of the greatest things that he ever said to me. He said, "I want to tell you something. You better get yourself together or you are not going to be around to help her while she is out there." I never ever thought about it like that and I thought, "Golly, he might be right." Butch loves Darlene. He helps me in a totally different way.

Dan told me that Terry was not happy about him moving in to an apartment with Darlene. I didn't tell Dan's dad. I thought this is what needs to be done and this is what Darlene and Dan want.

The Laundry

Dan would walk to the laundry room at the apartment complex to do their laundry. It was quite a distance from their apartment.

One day I got a phone call. Dan said, "Darlene came home from work and threw a pitcher at me because I lost a sock and a t-shirt." I went over to the apartment (you laugh now, but it wasn't funny then).

He put his hand up so the plastic pitcher wouldn't hit him and it cut his hand, he was bleeding. I said, "Darlene, you cannot do this kind of stuff. A sock and a t-shirt can be replaced. For crying out loud. Can you imagine what it takes to go up there and do the laundry? Would you want Dan to throw something at you? Dan could have called the police." Dan said, "Yeah Darlene, I could have called the cops." After this incident Darlene got better with dealing with things.

The entire time they lived in the efficiency apartment, they told me they wanted to get married. I told them it would be awhile before they could get married. All the time I was thinking, "Yeah right." Dan talked more about getting married than Darlene.

I Got a Job

Darlene and Dan's apartment allowed me the time to get a job outside the home.

I saw an ad in the newspaper for a part-time person to work in a pharmacy. I went in for an interview and after a week, the pharmacist called to let me know I had gotten the job. He knew I had a daughter with a disability and I had to drive her to and from work. He let me off when I needed to be off. I worked for him for 20 years and he was wonderful to work for.

Butch thought it was a good idea for me to get a job too so I could get my social security quarters in.

Apartment Two

After the first year they moved across the street, in the same apartment complex. The apartment was bigger and it had a washer and dryer.

At the new apartment there was one problem after another. The washer overflowed and caused water damage to the lower apartment and they had to pay for the repairs. The downstairs neighbors complained about the noise. In the morning, Dan would accidentally drop his razor on the floor and would slam the apartment door when going to work.

Darlene and Dan kept asking me, "When are you going to let us get married?" After they lived in the second apartment for a year, I thought their relationship was good and it was the right time to let them get married. So, I started to plan their wedding.

Agency Assistance

When Darlene and Dan moved into their first apartment, the Case Management Unit contracted to have a provider agency go out and check in on Darlene and Dan. The support person would take Darlene grocery shopping and would go into the apartment to make sure there was food to eat, the apartment was clean and the laundry was done.

The trash is what bothered me the most. Darlene and Dan lived in a second floor apartment and the trash would just pile up outside the door.

Darlene – "You'd have to walk down to the dumpster."

I would tell Darlene and Dan, "You cannot have this trash piled up like this. You need to get this trash down to the dumpster. What is it to walk down once a day? You have all the time in the world."

The support person from the agency got upset with me. She said, "Mom, the trash is none of your business. If there is a problem with the trash being piled up, it is the apartment complex's problem. You should not come here and talk to them like that."

Darlene - "I would probably get in trouble with the apartment complex about it."

The support person would take Darlene grocery shopping. Darlene didn't have the skills to plan a menu, make a grocery list and buy all the needed ingredients for recipes. Unfortunately, the lady was not teaching her. At the grocery store Darlene would just buy whatever she wanted except for candy, she wasn't allowed to buy candy.

The laundry would just pile up. I'd say, "Darlene, don't you think it's time to do some laundry?" She would just kinda look at me. I'd say, "Now Darlene, I am not coming over here and doing the laundry for you. That's part of living on your own. The next time I come back you better have the laundry done." The laundry would be done the next time I went back.

The support person also told me that I shouldn't be coming to the apartment to check the laundry.

I would go home and think, "I'm her MOTHER! I got Darlene this far!"

I could never talk to my youngest daughter, Anita, like I talk to Darlene and Dan. Darlene and Dan never complained about the way I talked to them and they learned through that. They always listen to what I need to say. To this day they seem to respect me for my advice. I am so grateful that they listen to me and want to please me.

Darlene – "I didn't like their equipment down there. I had a dishwasher that didn't work. The washing machine misfunctioned. I was doing laundry after ten o'clock at night and the thing over-flowed. The equipment wasn't right there."

Next, the support person called me on the phone and wanted me to hand over Darlene and Dan's checking and savings accounts.

I was the one who went with them to the bank to open their savings and checking accounts.

I was teaching them to save and to budget their money. That money was for them, they earned it.

I called the agency and told them, "I will not turn over the checking and savings accounts, I am just not going to do it." They said, "If you don't, we will have to drop the support services."

The services stopped immediately. Job support was separate, so they didn't lose that.

6
The Wedding

Dan's dad, Terry, told Dan he was wearing overalls to the wedding. Of course, this upset me because this was going to be a formal affair. So I called Terry on the phone and pleaded with him, "Can't you, for one day, for your son, dress in a suit?" Terry said, "Well, I'll give it some thought."

As the time got closer to the wedding Dan told me that Terry was taking his step mom to get a long dress for the wedding, so I knew Terry would wear a suit to the wedding.

Dan's family came and was very pleased with the wedding. Terry told me that he could not have come to anything nicer and that I did not miss a thing.

Dee, Dan's sister-in-law, told me how thankful she was that Dan found someone like Darlene to share his life with.

Darlene and Dan were married on March 31st, 1990.

7

Dan and Darlene Bought a House

Darlene and Dan saved their money. That's how they were able to buy this little home when it became available.

One day we got a flier in the mail from a real estate lady that we knew. There was a picture of a little house that was only a few blocks from where I live. There was a description of the interior and how much money would be needed for a down payment.

I was told that since Darlene and Dan received job support they could only have so much money in a savings and checking account. After reaching that dollar amount they would either lose their job support services or have to pay for them; they were allowed to own a house without affecting their job services.

Their money was accumulating and I didn't know what they were going to do with it. They couldn't give up their job support because I couldn't provide that service. Then, this home became available and they had enough money saved for a down payment.

The only difference between this house and the apartment was that they would have to pay their utilities and taxes themselves. I put it all down on paper and decided they could afford this home. This house was just perfect for them.

Butch felt things were just fine and Darlene and Dan should stay in their apartment.

We were out with Butch's brother and sister-in-law and we all stopped in to the open house. They thought the house was perfect and I thought the house was perfect, but Butch thought the apartment was good enough.

My son came to visit us that weekend and I took him down to see the house. It was not open so we just looked in the windows. My son thought buying the house was a good idea and he talked to Butch.

Butch's day off was Wednesday. He showed up at my place of work to see me, and he never came to work to see me, so I knew it was something important. He had gone to the bank to see if Darlene and Dan would qualify for a mortgage. The bank told him, as long as they had good credit they could get a mortgage. All we had to do was contact the real estate lady. I was very surprised because he did not tell me he was going to the bank. In fact, we didn't discuss the house at all after we went to the open house.

Nobody ever said there was a program to help people with intellectual disabilities buy a house. Nope, they bought that home just like you and me.

God had his hands in this.

8
Their Everyday Lives

Dan's Dad Died

I would take Dan to see Terry in the hospital because I thought it was the right thing to do.

Dan's Dad had been taking Dan back and forth from work. Transporting both Darlene and Dan to and from work is a lot, so it was a big help. After Terry got out of the hospital, I called him and asked him when he thought he'd get back to taking Dan to work. Dan's Dad said, "I don't think that I'll ever get back." I didn't realize how sick he was, he had leukemia.

Then we had a chat and he said," I cannot thank you enough for what you have done for Dan. I don't know what else to say to you. I never ever thought Dan would come as far as he has. I'd say to my second wife, Jean, we will have Dan forever and ever. Then the day came that Dan was not here. I have all the credit to give to you." I thought that was really nice. And now, Terry isn't around anymore.

Occasionally I ask Dan's step mother to do things to help me. If she can help me, she does. She is a very nice lady.

She took Dan to church with her until his days off were changed to Wednesday and Saturday.

She works part-time for Hershey Entertainment. We see her at Hershey Park and at the Hershey Bears hockey games. She also works at Hershey Theatre.

She knows I have it all under control and I guess I do.

I have contact with Darlene and Dan every day. When there is a problem they always call me.

911

On Dan's day off, he would walk to the local fire company. He was involved in fire house activities and had friends there.

When Darlene was at home she would call the fire house and ask to speak to Dan. Sometimes they called Dan to the phone and sometimes they didn't. Being the kind of person Darlene is, if they didn't let her speak to Dan, she would call back again, every five minutes or so.

Apparently she was dialing 911.

The fire chief said that if an emergency call came through and Darlene had the line tied up, the fire company could get in to a lot of trouble. So, the fire chief filed charges against Darlene and she got arrested. It was really an arrest. Her name appeared in the newspaper and she had to go to a hearing at the district justice's office.

This was a serious situation! I wish someone from the fire company would have come to talk to me about this, but they didn't. A customer at the pharmacy told me. Can you imagine!?

At the hearing the fire chief was adamant that the book be thrown at Darlene. The district justice wanted to handle the case within his office and kept asking the chief if he understood that Darlene had an intellectual disability. The chief said that he didn't care if she had an intellectual disability or not, he did not want her to call the fire company or come to the fire company, ever again. Everyone understood that there was going to be some kind of punishment. Back and forth it went. The district justice wanted to handle it out of his office, the chief wanted the book thrown at Darlene. Finally, the chief agreed to let the district justice handle it but said Darlene could never be on fire company property again. If she called the fire company she would have to be arrested.

It ended up that Darlene was on probation for six months.

So far, she has never called the fire company or gone on to the fire company property again.

Even today, Darlene gets emotional when she sees people from the fire company. I tell Darlene, "Those people are not your friends."

Darlene could have lost her job, ended up in jail, and had a permanent criminal record.

It all worked out.

Dan Gets Hurt

When Dan was off on the weekends he would walk to his friend's house just for something to do. This is the friend that use to take him to get his pay check cashed.

On his way home, I think he tripped and fell on the sidewalk. Somehow or other he struggled and got back to his house. He called me and said, "I fell and can't get up."

When I got there he was on the floor in the kitchen, his knee was swollen and he was in a lot of pain. I called the ambulance and they took him over to the Osteopathic Hospital.

It was bad, they had to operate and put screws in. I wasn't sure if he would ever go back to work because he stood to do his job.

After he came home, visiting nurses would come in to help him bathe and they sent him to physical therapy. He walked with a walker for a short time and when we went to the hockey games he needed to use a wheel chair.

After several months of recovery Dan was excited to return to work and his employer was glad to have him back.

I asked him how he liked being home and he said, "I was so bored."

Hockey – the Hershey Bears

Hockey has always been Butch's sport. When the kids were little we all went as a family. Sometimes Butch and I would leave the kids with a sitter and have a date night at the hockey game.

Our section is 125. Our seats are close to the floor of the rink, behind the glass. Darlene and Dan's seats are up in the corner section of 125.

Darlene and Dan have made friends in section 125.

Initially Darlene and Dan would buy their tickets at each game, but as their jobs became more secure they were able to buy half season passes.

Darlene and Dan are on their own at the stadium once we get to the games. They know where to meet us after the game.

Darlene – "I really enjoy my Bears, my Hershey Bears. I enjoy them. I enjoy hockey every year and I look to see if we can find a hockey trip to go on."

Darlene – "My hockey friends are so good to me and Dan. There was a table of them at the anniversary party. "

Darlene – "Each year at the hockey games, we don't eat supper there every time because that's twenty/twenty five dollars to eat at a hockey game and that gets expensive. "

Hershey Park

I take Darlene and Dan to Hershey Park a few times every year. We get season passes.

Darlene – "Hershey Park, I enjoy that, we got to the water park three times this year." (2015)

Speaking for Ourselves

How did you get involved with Speaking for Ourselves?

Darlene – "Janet Cambria got me and Dan into Speaking for Ourselves. She is the one who started this [Dauphin County] Speaking for Ourselves and worked with Dan Sausman. Next thing, she got sick and was out of the picture. Then Dan Sausman took over and then Richard came into the picture. "

Who was the President when you started in Speaking for Ourselves?

Darlene – "Jim White was the president when we started. Dan was the assistant president. Then after Jim left, Dan and I took it over. I'm thinking nine years. Yeah, there was an election, we voted. "

Darlene – "We needed a break from that, it was time to hand it over." (2015)

Commissioner Hartwick requested that the group discuss the importance of voting at 1 meeting each year. It has turned out to be a big event where preparation spans a few meetings. Each SFO member gets to tell everyone why they vote and usually at least 1 elected official comes to talk to the group.

Cruise Vacations

Darlene and Dan love going on cruises, we have taken them on five cruises.

Cruises are a perfect vacation for Darlene and Dan. I can easily keep tabs on them and I don't need to worry about them handling money.

We have had good cruise vacations with family and friends.

Church

Darlene and Dan are very involved in the church. Darlene and Dan's church friends are my friends, too.

Community Self –Advocacy

Both Darlene and Dan are self-advocates in the community. Their list of accomplishments are impressive. To name a few but not all....

- Darlene was pictured on an AHEDD brochure
- My Life, My Way panel discussions for the Partnership; the Partnership was affiliated with the Institute on Disabilities at Temple University
- Events and rallies at the state capital
- Freedom March
- Featured in a Central Penn Business Journal article; Hiring Employees with Disabilities, Pays Off for Local Employers
- Performed interviews for the Center for Independent Living
- Received the AHEDD Central Pennsylvania Living Well With a Disability Award
- Officers for Speaking for Ourselves
- Featured in a Patriot News article; Those with Mental Retardation Push Awareness of Voting Rights
- Received the Dauphin County Administrators Award for being the President of Speaking for Ourselves

Football

They are both football fans and watch the games on TV together. Darlene's team is the Dallas Cowboys and Dan's team is the Philadelphia Eagles. They occasionally go to the Middletown High School football games, too.

Darlene – "We bicker during the games. It's fun."

9

Darlene and Dan's 25th Wedding Anniversary

The Party – March 31, 2015

This was special, no ifs, ands, or buts about it.

My husband and I worked on Darlene and Dan's 25th wedding anniversary party, together.

Butch made the invitations and RSVP cards on the computer and he made the photo CD that was projected onto the large screens in the community room of the church.

One hundred and sixty nine people were on the invitation list.

There was a simple church service and they gave each other new rings as symbols of their renewed vows.

Featured speakers at the reception were Dan Sausman, from the Dauphin County Case Management Unit and Gerry Miner, from AHEDD.

I think Darlene was eight years old when I met Dan Sausman at the Case Management Unit. I can still see this young man sitting behind his desk and I thought, "What does this young guy know about kids." But I still listened to what he had to say, in fact I still listen to him today.

Gerry Miner was both Darlene and Dan's job coach, for at least 13 years, until her retirement in 2015.

Darlene – "I was very happy about the party. Dan and I were married twenty five years. That was the best day of my life and I'm going to get twenty five more years in. I thought, well, I had a nice man there and I thought he would treat me well. "

Darlene – "A lot of people came. There was one hundred and forty some. I was upset because nobody from my work came, they said they were coming, I was a little upset, and they didn't come. I can understand that the general manager didn't come."

Darlene - "I was happy that my friends from Speaking for Ourselves came. Terry and Mary came, Stephanie came, Richard came, and Dan Sausman came. Everything was great. "

Dan Sausman's Speech

Happy 25th Wedding Anniversary, Dan & Darlene!

It is an honor to be included in the celebration of your 25th wedding anniversary and the recommitment of your vows. You have accomplished, through your strength of your marriage, what so many people have tried and where so many have failed.

I am privileged to call you friends. In reflecting on what I would say to you today, many thoughts flooded my mind, but what kept coming back to me over and over was the word, inspiration. Not that a 25th wedding anniversary isn't inspiration enough, but you have accomplished so much, and have inspired others in so many ways. What you have accomplished isn't inspirational because of your disabilities, it is inspirational because of your capabilities!

Vince Lombardi, the legendary coach of the Green Bay Packers at their zenith, said; "The measure of who we are is what we do with what we have." Darlene and Dan, what you have accomplished is a testament to the truth of Coach Lombardi's wisdom!

Let's just take a minute to reflect on just some of these accomplishments –

Not just celebrating your 25th wedding anniversary, but recommitting to each other in the truest expression of love and devotion.

- Holding down jobs, the same jobs, for nearly 30 years each...28 for Darlene and 29 for Dan: that's an accomplishment for anyone to be proud of! You have been productive and contributing. And yes, tax paying citizens.

- Owning your own home...a home that you have paid off through your own labor; another incredible accomplishment for anyone. Many strive to purchase a home let alone own their home outright!

- Living life fully – being the world's greatest Hershey Bears fans, going on trips and cruises, Hershey Park.

- Being connected to your community. Whether cheering on the Middletown High School football team or helping out a neighbor.

- And then there's Speaking for Ourselves (SFO). Since the Central PA Chapter was chartered in 2004 you both have dedicated yourselves and given so much to the Central PA Chapter. The Chapter wouldn't be where it is today without your commitment, leadership and energy. As charter members, you have been a driving force behind this grassroots self-advocacy group that is run by and for people with developmental disabilities. In fact, you were there before the beginning. Leaders among a small group of self-advocates who began meeting two years before to plant the seed. You have helped the group grow into a strong, vibrant and productive organization. You have accomplished many things through your leadership and participation in SFO. Although there are too many to cover completely, I will take a moment to touch on just a few;

  ♦ You have helped to triple the membership of the Chapter. You now have almost 35 members who attend monthly chapter meetings on a regular basis. This is an accomplishment that is almost unheard of among self-advocacy groups. In fact, even the statewide self-advocacy group, Self-Advocates United as One (SAU1) visited recently and their coordinator was incredibly impressed and awed by the size and energy of your Chapter.

  ♦ You led the group as officers for many years and now support the new leadership in a manner that is gracious, supportive and a model for any transition of leadership in any organization, anywhere!

♦ You have connected with the Dauphin County Board of Commissioners, Commissioner Hartwick in particular, through the Voter Education and Registration Forums that you have supported through SFO. I attended an event in March in recognition of Developmental Disabilities Awareness Month where Commissioner Hartwick spoke. He mentioned the SFO group in his comments.

♦ You have made connections in the community and shared the benefits of those connections for the benefit of SFO. John Wilsbach helped the chapter professionally record their mission statement and outreach message. Former Bears coach, Mark French, visited the chapter twice; the first time at your request the second time at his request, he was so impressed with the group – wow!

♦ You marched at The Capitol through the statewide Freedom March to advocate for supports and services for individuals with developmental disabilities.

♦ You participated in statewide training through The Partnership. You told individuals and families about the incredible accomplishments you have achieved in your lives. You inspire others to dream and believe that they too can aspire to those things in their own lives.

♦ I could go on and on, literally, but I think these highlights begin to paint the picture of why inspiration comes to my mind when I think about you both.

- I came to know you both when I was the SFO coordinator. This was a connection that has been more meaningful and enriching to me than I can begin to express. The inspiration that I feel has come not only from what you have accomplished, but from the people you are:

  ♦ Dan – I could think of no better leader to have brought SFO to where it is today. You are SFO's greatest cheerleader. You always promote SFO and talk to anyone you can about how great the organization is. You work a room better than most politicians. I have always been impressed with your confidence and openness as I watched you approach people, introduce yourself and speak on behalf of SFO. All that on top of you being one of the most truly decent, kind, caring and open people that I have ever had the pleasure to know.

  ♦ Darlene – your energy and drive has given much more to the chapter than anyone knows. I joke that you're my toughest boss, but in reality, I deeply appreciate knowing how on top of things you are when it comes to Chapter meetings. When things were so busy and my mind is going in many directions, I knew I could always count on your calls and reminders to keep me focused on preparations needed for the next chapter meeting or event. I appreciate those calls, it made a huge difference! You have been an example and a teacher to me. I often comment to other professionals about the power and energy of our SFO members. I especially remember a meeting quite some time ago where we discussed assignments. At most meetings, when it comes time to discuss assignments and seek volunteers, most eyes look down or away and many folks do what they can to avoid the extra duty. But not you Darlene. Your hand shot up right away, but what I really remember is asking if you could volunteer for two things. You reassured me that you could handle both. I'll always remember that moment with admiration and respect. If more people were like you, the world would be a much better place.

So, I conclude by saying, congratulations on your 25 years of marriage and wishing you many, many more. And I thank you both, and your family, for your friendship, and continued inspiration.

10

Life Today – 2016

Home Life

$\mathcal{D}$arlene and Dan paid their house off in 23 years. In months where there were 3 pays instead of 2, they made an extra payment.

After the house was paid for it was time for a new roof and some updates inside the house.

Butch suggested that they apply for a home equity loan to pay for the repairs. Darlene and Dan went to the bank to apply for the loan. Their credit was excellent and the loan was quickly approved. Of course, Darlene and Dan signed their own paperwork.

While the improvements were being done they decided that a carport would be a nice addition. It looks very nice and protects them in bad weather.

Dan has his TV in a bedroom (man cave) and Darlene has her TV in the living room.

Money Management

Darlene gets a paper check on payday and walks to the bank to cash it. Dan has his check directly deposited.

They still save a little, spend a little on things they want, and they have bills automatically withdrawn from their accounts. On a rare occasion Darlene writes a check. I keep a very small amount of their money with me for emergencies, clothes, and outings.

Darlene - "I have been doing better with my money."

Darlene - "At the grocery store I had $70.00 to spend and I went over to $83.00. I had $20.00 extra setback for groceries."

Darlene – "I use to spend that extra money. I'd go to the dollar store and buy lip balm and little packs of tissues and little purses."

Darlene - "Mom would say this is your hard earned money. You don't need 6 or 12 of these."

Darlene gets better and better every day. I just work with her, going over and over.

Driving

Darlene and Dan never got their drivers licenses. Darlene tried a few times but was never successful.

Transportation has always been a commitment. My husband and I have always taken them to and from work, doctors' appointments, dentist appointments, grocery shopping, activities, etc. Whatever the need we were always there to provide transportation.

Meal Preparation and House-Keeping

Darlene is on the ball with meal preparation. She decides what she is going to prepare, makes a grocery list and does the shopping by herself. She has a food budget and that's the amount of money that she spends.

Darlene – "I have been putting money back for food."

Darlene has learned to cook in the oven, microwave, and crock pot. She does not use the stove top. She is very confident cooking like this and does a good job. Sometimes, I still help Darlene with meal planning.

Darlene is a good housekeeper. She keeps everything neat and clean. She does the laundry as soon as a load accumulates and separates the lights from the darks. Darlene didn't do the laundry when she lived at my house so she learned this when she left home.

There were times after Darlene and Dan bought their home that I would have to tell Darlene it was time to do the laundry. Now, I don't have to say anything to her. I don't even have to look to see if there is laundry. It is all routine now.

Darlene – "Yeah, I would let the laundry pile up. Now, as soon as I get a pile of dirty clothes, I just do a load of wash. As soon as I get a load of lights and a load of darks I get them in."

Dishes are done on a regular basis. Darlene will call me to tell me that they ate and the dishes are all cleaned up.

It's all routine now. She never would have learned any of it had she lived at my house.

She has learned all that.

There was a time when I thought Darlene would always be with me.

The Holidays

We go to Anita's house for Christmas, the Sunday after Christmas everyone goes to Jeffrey's house and I have everyone for Thanksgiving.

In 2014 we all went to Darlene and Dan's house for Christmas. Anita got Dan an Xbox for his TV and Anita's boyfriend hooked it up.

Darlene was thrilled that everyone came to her house.

Darlene and Dan decorate their own Christmas tree.

Darlene - "Last year I thought for sure we'd get a gift card from Jeff, but he went online and got me a Dallas Cowboy jacket and got Dan an Eagles jacket. We really like them. We bicker when the teams play. Anita got Dan Xbox for his TV."

Darlene and Dan give Darlene's niece's gift cards for Christmas and Darlene addressed all the cards herself. If I line a task out she can do it and things go fine.

Time Management

I raised Darlene to be very prompt and she is still prompt, today. If I am two minutes late, Darlene calls me and says, "You are two minutes late, you said five o'clock."

Dan was very impatient when he worked. In the morning, before work, if he didn't have to be to work until 7:00 a.m., he would call us when he woke up, not when he was ready to go, but when he woke up. When the phone would ring in the morning, we knew it was Dan.

We have always had Darlene and Dan to work on time. If we were not waiting for them when work was over, they would call us immediately.

If we want to take them somewhere that has not been previously scheduled, the only thing they want to know is if they will have enough time to get ready?

They are very punctual.

Computers

Today, any paperwork that can be done online is done on the computer.

Butch does all their computer stuff for them.

Summer Camp

Dan has been going to summer camp for years, but Darlene has just started to go the past few years.

They like to take pictures so I always send a throw away camera with them.

Their church pays for half of the camp fee and Darlene and Dan pay for the other half. The church will pay half even if you are not a member of the church.

Church

Our church is family to Darlene and Dan. They are very well accepted there and well liked there.

Health Issues

At the age of fifty two Dan was diagnosed with Parkinsons disease.

Darlene - "I help him with his medication. He gets mixed up."

We first noticed that Dan would be confused when we would go to unfamiliar places. If we would go to a restaurant and he had to go to the bathroom, he would not be able to find his way back to the table by himself.

Dan always rode along to pick Darlene up from work. He would stand at the corner, a few houses down from their house, and I would pick him up. Cold weather started to bother him and he doesn't want to wait in the cold anymore.

On Dan's day off he started to compulsively eat a lot of food. To test if he was really hungry or not I took him to breakfast and he ate 3 pancakes and sausage. As soon as he got home he had to have more to eat. He wasn't hungry, he was just eating compulsively.

When talking about his work day, he always says that he did really good, but the job coach would tell us differently.

When his supervisor would ask him if he completed a task Dan just started saying, "Yes" to everything. Sometimes he had completed the task, but other times he did not. He would forget to do some of his normal routine tasks.

We all felt that he was not intentionally lying. He truly thought that he did do a good job.

Some of that has to be frustrating for his employer too. As it turns out, his employer was more than willing to work with Dan to maintain his employment.

Right after the diagnosis I wanted Dan to go to a day program, five days a week. Everyone else, i.e. his employer, his job coach, Case Management and Butch all said that he should work as long as he can.

The doctor prescribed medicine and his employer bought a new dish washer and for a while he did much better.

I told Dan, that there would come a day when he wouldn't go to work anymore, he would go to a day program instead. Dan has a really good attitude and said, "Well I don't know why I wouldn't like the program." He wanted to know if he would still live at his and Darlene's house, if he would still be able to go to hockey games and if he would still be able to go to Hershey Park. I told him, "Yes, you will still be able to do all those things." (Doesn't this make you want to cry?)

Things have progressed to the point where everyone was in agreement. Dan will be retiring on January 10th of 2016. He says, "I am done" and seems happy that he is retiring. He looks tired.

Dan's Last Day at Work

Dan was employed at the Compass Group/Canteen/Con-Ven-Co for a total of 30 years. The supervisors and the employees all treated Dan nicely and with respect, he had a great work experience there and was happy; the company became Dan's work family. He has many friends from working there and will never forget all those working years and friendships.

I am very thankful and grateful for the people at Con-Ven-Co. They were flexible and cooperative to work with.

On his last day at work, while performing his normal job duties, water backed up in the drain and shot out of the drain. Dan became disoriented, fell, and broke his hip.

He was taken to the hospital and had to have surgery to repair the hip and he went to rehab after the surgery. At his last orthopedic visit he was switched over to a cane from a walker.

Dan was very disappointed that he missed his retirement party and cake.

11

What About Butch and Me?

Normal Bickering

*W*hen Butch and I are together, by ourselves, we are fine. I think it is the stress of taking care of two. Darlene is pretty self-sufficient except she says things two or three times. Dan needs a lot more help than Darlene, especially after his accident, but he will get better and improve. Butch and I bicker about everything......ahh. I think that's normal.

What Do Butch and I Do Together

On Wednesdays Butch and I use to go out to eat, walk through the mall or drive to Lancaster for ice cream.

We have been on thirty five cruises together without Darlene and Dan.

We no longer go to an eight to five job, but there is always all this other stuff to do. We are far from being retired, at least what most people envision as retirement.

Lately, we have not been doing anything together.

Our 50th Wedding Anniversary

Our 50th wedding anniversary was March 13th, 2015.

I really wanted to have a big celebration, but when I sat down and started to make our invitation list, I realized Butch and I didn't have many mutual friends. The people on the list were friends of mine and Darlene and Dan. So, I decided not to plan a party.

Our entire family got together for dinner; Anita and her family, Jeffrey and his family, Darlene and Dan, and Butch and I. They bought us tickets to a show and dinner at Lancaster's Dutch Apple Theater.

Now We Get Paid

It's easier now that I am retired from the pharmacy and Butch is retired from the post office. We are so called retired but there is always all this other stuff to do.

The first thing I asked Butch to do when he retired was transport either Darlene or Dan to and from work. It's a big help to me. Sometimes we switch and sometimes he transports both Darlene and Dan.

Some people would say, "Well, there is a bus that could take Darlene to and from work" and they were right. Darlene would have to be at the bus stop at 6:30 in the morning, then in to the square in Harrisburg to transfer to another bus that goes to the Harrisburg Mall. Then, she'd have to pick up a van that transports hotel guests to and from the Harrisburg Mall, I'm not even sure if the hotel does that anymore. I let Darlene try it a few times and I worried the whole time. I have always transported her to and from work. I have peace of mind knowing she is there on time and safe.

When I worked at the pharmacy, and Butch was still working at the post office, I was taking both Darlene and Dan to and from work. I'd get up early to get Dan off to work, then I'd go back home and do a few things, then I'd take Darlene to work, then I'd go to work. I was exhausted before I even got to work. For a while, Dan's dad was helping me but then he got sick and died.

Approximately three years ago (2011 or 2012, I was sixty seven) the county supports coordinator was at Darlene and Dan's house for their yearly visit. The supports coordinator was not their regular supports coordinator. I arrived late. When I got there, I described my day. The supports coordinator said, "You did all that, today?" I said, "Yes" and she said, "I hope you are getting paid for that." Then she said, "Darlene and Dan can hire someone to take them to and from work and to run errands and to go on occasional outings." I said, "I don't know what you are talking about, I have been doing this for years and years."

I said to Darlene, go call your Daddy and ask him to come over here and listen to this. I didn't want to get into something that would cost us money or get money that we would have to pay back later. If I would tell Butch what the supports coordinator told me he wouldn't believe me. Butch came over and the supports coordinator explained all this to us. It had to be written into their individual support plan and into their budget. The fact that they are on their own, we are entitled. I never knew there was a program like this.

I am only paid when Darlene is in the car or when Dan is in the car. When I take them to work I am paid, but I'm not paid for the trip back home when they are not in the car.

I look at how many years we transported them for nothing.

We are eligible only because they are out there living on their own. If they lived with us, we would not be eligible. That's what we were told. Butch questioned it numerous times. It just doesn't seem right, but it is. You take the good with the bad. It does help with the gas money. I learned all this through Case Management.

Before, I didn't let an agency take over their bank accounts, so why would I let someone else drive them to and from work or take them to the grocery store? I wouldn't know who it is.

I could hardly believe it when I got the paycheck the first time. I just looked at this check as my retirement.

I have a lot of faith in God. I worked part-time for 20 years at a pharmacy. The reason I stayed at the pharmacy was because my boss gave me the flexibility I needed. I worked and he paid me and gave me vacation days. I paid into social security, but I didn't have any other benefits.

When I did decide to retire and take my social security at 62, I saw what I was getting and I was grateful to have it. I could not believe that I put in all those years and this is all the money I'm going to get. I kind of felt like I missed out on something since I didn't have a pension, but I have Darlene and Dan and look at where they are and what they have accomplished.

Butch has good government benefits that I was included in. You go through life and don't think a pension is very important. I told Butch that he'd have to keep me for the rest of my life because I cannot live on my social security.

12

In Conclusion

$\mathcal{D}$an is a great and wonderful son-in-law. Darlene could not have found a better mate and I do not know where each would be without the other. Dan tells me, frequently, that his mother would have been so happy to know he has someone like me and Darlene to help him in his life. I sincerely believe Darlene and Dan's marriage was in God's plan for them. My dad and brother told me, the day Darlene and Dan got married, it was a marriage made in heaven.

Darlene and Dan would never have learned or accomplished what they have had they not been given the opportunity. They are great individuals and I am proud of them.

Darlene and Dan are my life accomplishments and my life's rewards. I have accomplished my goal in life to teach Darlene to be as independent, successful and safe to the best of her ability. Through her success and confidence she has accomplished what we worked so hard to gain. And, Dan was her friend beside her the whole way.

I will take care of Darlene and Dan for as long as I can because they are part of me.

13

What Will Happen When....?

My boss at the pharmacy used to ask me, "What will happen when....?"

Well, I'm not sure ....

I pray that I will live ....

Darlene and Dan both have retirement accounts that they can start to collect at fifty nine and a half. Darlene has eleven years to go. Dan had eight years to go, but he got sick and can't work anymore ....

If something goes wrong over at the house, she doesn't have any knowledge of who to call ....

I won't be there to transport them back and forth to and from work anymore ....

I would hope that my son or daughter would help, but Anita has her hands full with her own family and Jeffrey lives in New Jersey ....

I've been trying to say to myself, she knows the difference between right and wrong ....

Dan has more common sense and is calmer about things than the average person ....

I think Darlene will be fine ....

I feel Darlene and Dan are as independent as they are going to get.

CPSIA information can be obtained at www.ICGtesting.com
Printed in the USA
BVOW06*2253290716

457225BV00001B/1/P